Contents

Paul →

← Jane

What's on the menu?

What kind of food do you choose to eat? Do you choose food that is good for you, or any food as long as you like the taste? You can try to choose tasty food that is good for you and good for the planet, and become part of the Green Team!

Good for you

A healthy diet

In order to be healthy and fit, we need to eat a good mix of foods. Food can be put into five groups. All of these groups are important for the body, and a balanced diet is one that includes all the food groups.

We need to eat more food from some of these food groups than others. Use the plate on the right to get the balance right in what you eat. The smaller the section on the plate, the less you need of that type of food.

Fruit and vegetables provide:

- vitamins
- minerals
- carbohydrates
- fibre.

Bread, cereal, rice, potato and pasta give us

- carbohydrates, the food your body uses for energy.
- B vitamins
- some calcium
- iron
- fibre.

Meat, fish and pulses (beans) give us:

- protein
- iron
- vitamins
- minerals.

Foods containing fat and sugar give us energy but we should not eat too much of these types of food.

Milk and dairy products give us:

- calcium
- vitamins
- protein.

These children are enjoying a healthy school lunch.

Challenge!

- Is the food you choose to eat every day good for you?
- What can you do to improve it?

Good for the planet

To join the Green Team you also need to make sure you eat food that has been properly prepared and is good for the world around you as well as tasty to eat.

Fairtrade

Cheap food for us can mean the farmer's family goes hungry. Food that carries the Fairtrade label means that the farmer who produced it will have been paid a fair amount of money.

Organic food

Chemicals that kill bugs can kill plants and animals too. Choose food grown without dangerous chemicals.

Food miles

Some food has travelled from the other side of the world for you to eat. You can choose food grown near where you live and help to cut down food miles.

Packaging

Choose food that comes without much packaging, or in packaging that can be reused, recycled or will rot down quickly.

Action!

Find out if your school lunches are good for the planet. Is the food:

• fairtrade?

• organic?

• local and seasonal?

If not, help your school to make changes.

Giang

Time for a picnic?

If you are planning a picnic or taking a lunch box to school, think before you pack your food and drink. Use washable containers you can use again and again so you don't have to keep throwing away packaging.

Energy is used to make unnecessary packaging. It has to be thrown away. Then more energy is used to get rid of the packaging.

Fruit and vegetables come in their own natural wrapping.

Challenge!

- Collect all the packaging used in your class's lunch boxes for a week.
- Now go for a week trying not to use any wrapping that can't be reused, recycled or put in the compost bin.
- Compare the piles of packaging for the two weeks.
- Keep up the challenge and reduce packaging week by week. Can you get it down to zero?

Fruit and vegetables

You can either eat the skin of fruit and vegetables or peel it and put it in the compost bin.

Result – no waste!

Drink tap water rather than bottled water to cut down on packaging.

Drinks

Buy a big container of milk or juice instead of lots of small ones. Pour some into a washable, reusable bottle for your picnic or packed lunch.

Sandwich box

Put your sandwiches in a small container in your lunch box. Or fill it with home-made coleslaw, pasta or rice salad for a change.

Yogurt pot

Get a reusable pot for your deserts. Fill it with stewed fruit and honey or yogurt from a big container.

 # Action!

Make your own picnic lunch

Bake flapjacks, oat biscuits or banana bread (see below) and brown bread rolls

Stew fruit with honey.

Make more than you need for one meal. Freeze or store the extra food or share with friends.

◆ Remember to ask for adult help when baking

Banana bread

Preparation time less than 30 mins
Cooking time 1 to 2 hours

Ingredients
225g/8oz self-raising flour
110g/4oz butter
120g/5oz caster sugar
450g/1lb Fairtrade bananas (the softer the better), peeled and mashed
½ tsp salt
2 eggs
175g/6oz mixed dried fruit

Method
1. Pre-heat the oven to 180°C/350°F/Gas 4.
2. Mix all the ingredients except the dried fruit together.
3. Add the dried fruit. Spoon into a non-stick loaf tin, spread evenly and bake it for one-and-a-half hours.
4. Cool on a wire rack, then slice and serve!

School meals in Ghana

It's difficult to work hard at school if you are hungry or if the food you eat isn't good for you. The Tibung school in Ghana, Africa, is working to provide pupils with healthy meals that are also good for the local environment and the planet.

Case study – School meals at the Tibung school

The pupils at Tibung school in Ghana, Africa have made a commitment to eat in a green way. They eat maize, yam, rice, okra and meat from local farms. Eggs, tomatoes and onions are brought in from the nearest town.

School children wait for school lunch in Tibung, Ghana.

Sylvia

10-year-old Sylvia says:

"My favourite food is rice and beans! The portions of the meals we get in school are big enough, but I finish it all! In my class we have about 36 children and we eat the meals in our classroom."

School feeding programme

The Dutch organisation SIGN is donating money to schools in Ghana, such as Tiburg, to help them provide hot meals for school children. The children get a healthy meal and the food is provided by local farmers.

Challenge!

Find out where the food for school lunches comes from. Ask your school to buy as much food as possible from local farmers or farmers' markets if you live in an urban area. The food is often organic, which is better for you and the environment.

Gladys

The whole school can help make meals healthy and green.

Write a letter to your headteacher to try to persuade him or her to only buy local, healthy produce for school dinners.

Gladys Abaa, teacher at Tibung school says:

"I eat with the children in the classroom. The food is nutritious and good, and it encourages children to come to school… the attention of the children is also better!"

From farm to fork

Local farmer Francis Kwaku will provide Tiburg school with rice, maize and groundnuts.

Francis says:

Francis

"I sell my produce to the markets nearby. My farm is located approximately 12 km from the school, where one of my children is going to as well."

A school shop

Healthy snacks help to give you energy so choose healthy snacks at home and at school. Some schools run eco-friendly shops selling healthy snacks to pupils to help keep them going all day long.

Healthy tuck shops

If your school has a garden you can grow fruit and vegetables to sell at the school shop. The money you make can go towards looking after the garden.

Mossbank School in Shetland sells food grown at the school to pupils. These treats were made for Halloween.

Chocolate

Dora

Cola

Crisps

Crisps

Dora has replaced crisps, chocolate and cans of fizzy drink with healthy snacks such as fruit that don't come in packaging.

This poster has a catch phrase to help sell the food on offer. Think of some more catchy phrases to sell your tuck shop food.

Running a shop

Buy fruit and vegetables from local farmers and Fairtrade suppliers.
Sell whole fruit, fruit slices, cups of vegetable sticks, home-made smoothies and banana bread (see page 9).

Smoothie recipe

- Half a blender of fruit juice or a quarter juice and a quarter milk
- 1 peeled, chopped banana
- A handful of other chopped fruit
- Add a little honey or yogurt

Whiz it all up together and enjoy a healthy drink.

Challenge!

Run your own school tuck shop

Give everyone at school the chance to snack on healthy, eco-friendly food.

Promoting your shop

Make posters to promote the tuck shop. Make sure it tells people about the delicious and healthy snacks on offer, and about the eco-benefits of the shop.

Action!

Do some market research.

Send out a questionnaire to parents, governors, staff and pupils

- Would you buy snacks from a school shop?
- How much would you pay for a snack?
- What would you like to eat?

Use the answers to decide how to set up the tuck shop.

Choose suppliers of local, organic or Fairtrade fruit and vegetables.

A school garden

All around the world, schools are creating their own gardens. Schools grow healthy food to cook and eat and sometimes even have enough left over to sell and make money for looking after their garden. Making sure their gardens are eco-friendly has helped many schools to become eco-schools. Rockland Primary are a great example of an eco-school.

Zita

At Rocklands Primary, a small school in Mitchell's Plain, South Africa, teacher Mrs Zita Cheemee and her pupils have created a fantastic vegetable and wildlife garden. Every morning children water the plants, weed the garden and empty leftover food into a composting "bath".

Food from your own garden doesn't need extra packaging.

Action!

Eat healthily and help to look after your environment.

- Grow your own fruit and vegetables.
- Food from your own garden doesn't have far to travel to your plate.
- Recycle food waste to make your own compost.
- Avoid using chemicals by controlling pests naturally. Onions, garlic and chillies will do the job.
- Save water by collecting rainwater to water the garden.

To teach students about how their food choices affect their health, the environment, and the community, chef Alice Waters created The Edible School Garden at Martin Luther King Junior Middle School, California, USA.
Pupils learn in an organic garden and kitchen classroom.

Case study – The edible school garden

To make a change from buying food in the supermarket, the Martin Luther King Junior Middle School, California, USA has created an edible school garden. The children sow the seeds and look after the growing plants.

Pupils learn about healthy eating and caring for the environment. They get plenty of outdoor fun and exercise at the same time.

Local and seasonal food

It is possible to grow food in most parts of the world all year round. You won't need a greenhouse or extra lighting, heating and water for seasonal crops to thrive. They will be extra tasty too.

Challenge!

You can harvest food from your garden all year round.

When you are planning your school garden, find out which fruit and vegetables grow well where you live and the best time to plant and harvest them.

Here are some popular vegetables. Find out when you have to sow and harvest them:

- Leeks
- Purple sprouting broccoli
- Peas
- Pumpkin
- Strawberries
- Tomatoes.

How far has it travelled?

The food on this plate comes from all over the world. The vegetables come from Spain and Kenya, the potatoes from America and the beef comes from Argentina. Where does your food come from?

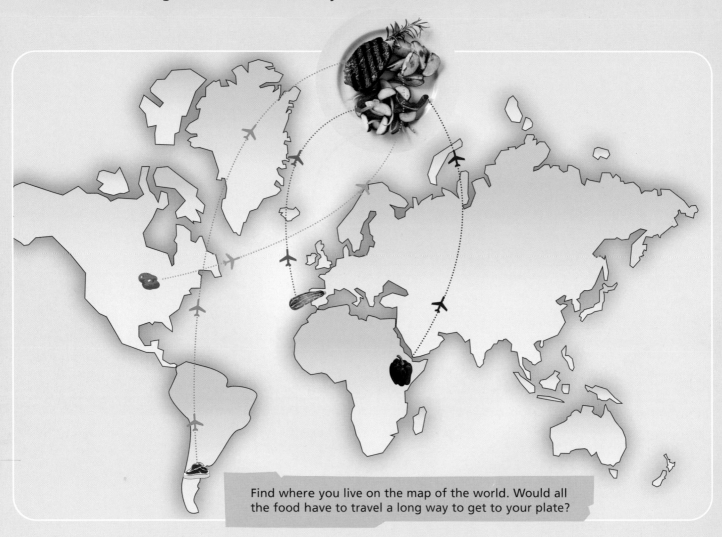

Find where you live on the map of the world. Would all the food have to travel a long way to get to your plate?

Food miles

Food miles are the distance food has to travel from the farm to your plate. Much of the food we eat travels from place to place by air, sea and land. The further food has to travel, the more fuel is used and the more damage to the environment is caused.

Local markets

In many places in the world, farmers bring their food to sell at the local market. Most of the customers come on foot because they live nearby. Food from the market doesn't have far to travel to make a delicious meal of fresh food to put on the table.

Challenge!

Work out the food miles.

- Add up the food miles of your own lunch.
- Add up the food miles of your friend's lunch.
- Which of you can change your lunch and have the fewest food miles?

Go to **www.organiclinker.com/food-miles** for a food miles calculator.

Eric →

Eric lives in New York. The bread in his lunch box was made from wheat grown in Minnesota, the apple came from Florida and the peanuts from South Africa. What is the food mileage on his lunch? How could he improve it?

At this market in Tanzania, women sell the vegetables they grow on their smallholdings.

Action!

Cutting down food miles

- Walk to the shops to buy your food.
- Whenever you can, buy local food. Shop at a farmers' market.
- Find out where food comes from and how far it has travelled.
- Find out if your school meals are cooked from local, fresh food. If not, see if you can make changes.

Get cooking!

Food you have grown yourself tastes especially good. If you have a garden at home, ask if you can have a small patch to grow vegetables. Treat your family to a meal you have cooked with vegetables from your garden.

Case study – Nunawading school

Nunawading School in Australia works with the Stephanie Alexander Kitchen Garden Foundation to encourage children to grow, harvest, prepare and share their own food.

Challenge!

Find out what you can grow where you live so you have fresh food all year round.

- Grow it.
- Harvest it.
- Learn how to cook it.
- Eat it!

1. Vegetables such as runner beans, tomatoes and courgettes are grown in the school garden by pupils.

Aaron, 7, says:

"I love planting vegetables and watching them grow through the year. Best of all is when we get to pick them and make delicious meals from them. It is good to know where our food comes from."

2. Pupils then pick the produce and take it into the kitchen, supervised by adults.

3. Delicious meals are then served up to the rest of the school year.

Weerayut

Weerayut, 10, says:

"I enjoy working in the vegetable garden. Thanks to this project, I have learnt about vegetables, how to grow them and to look after chickens. My family now ask for my advice and help and I know I can contribute."

Case study – A vegetable garden in Thailand

The Ban-Daeng school in Mahasarakham, Thailand, has more than 150 students and serves five neighbouring villages. The school, local farmers and the charity Plan International have introduced a vegetable garden and farm into the school.

Using the vegetables

Through the management of the school vegetable garden and a small farm, the students learnt how to raise livestock and grow vegetables. The fresh produce is used to prepare healthy lunches for the students, reducing the malnutrition rate. The remainder of the produce is sold to market sellers and community members.

The pupils of Ban-Daeng school in Thailand made a delicious pak choi salad using local ingredients.

Action!

Get cooking!

Make a delicious salad like the one on the right using fresh, ingredients from your local area.

Crispy lettuce, spring onions, peas and apple make up this crispy green salad.

Mini gardens

Your home might not have a garden and lots of city schools don't have space for a garden. But you can grow all kinds of different fruit and vegetables in window boxes, pots, hanging-baskets and containers.

What can you grow?

You can grow almost anything. Start with food you like to eat. Grow just one or two kinds of vegetable at first. When you get good at it, try something new.

These old tyres have been used for growing potatoes!

Some vegetables such as chives can be grown in very small spaces.

Inside and outside

Window sills are a good place for growing small pots of herbs. Sunlight shines through the glass and you can open the windows for some fresh air. Remember to water the pots. The rain can't do the job for you inside!

Outside, unused containers can act as a place for growing food. Old tyres, pots and even wellington boots all act as an ideal home for all kinds of plants.

Challenge!

Use your imagination

Don't buy new containers, re-use what you already have:

• half an old football for a hanging basket
• plastic storage boxes
• baskets
• old boots.

The container must:

• be big enough for the fully grown plant
• have holes for water to drain.

Fill it with eco-friendly soil.
Use home-made compost (see pages 22-23).

Seeds can be planted in any container, from an old football to a hanging basket.

Action!

Prepare a container.

• Punch holes for drainage.
• Add light soil. Make sure it is clean and fresh. Try to use soil without peat (see page 23).
• Water the soil.
• Plant a young vegetable or fruit plant.
• If your container is light, you can move it to protect it from the hot sun or a frost.

Looking after containers

Containers need some shelter and some sunshine. They can stand against a wall or fence. Put them near to a tap so you can water them easily and keep your gardening tools handy. If you are using a window box make sure it is firmly fixed to the window sill.

Pete

Children at Pete's school in London take the containers home and water the vegetables at weekends and in the holidays.

Compost

Soil is made up of tiny bits of rock, dead plants and animals. Plants take goodness from the soil to feed them as they grow. Soil that is used for growing vegetables over and over again loses some of its goodness. It needs feeding with good quality compost.

You can make your own compost at home or at school. The children at Rocklands Primary in South Africa have created a compost "bath", and use earthworms to turn leftover food into great compost.

What is compost?

Compost is decayed plants and other natural things such as tea leaves or fruit and vegetable peelings. It is added to soil to make the soil richer.

Compost helps keep soil full of the goodness plants need to grow healthily. You can add some kinds of school lunch leftovers to your school compost heap.

Why is a compost heap green?

Compost heaps:
• reduce waste
• recycle food
• make natural compost
• help vegetables to grow
• you eat the vegetables and grow strong and healthy.

Fruit and vegetables, like these old pumpkins, make great compost.

What can be made into compost?

• Uncooked fruit and vegetable leftovers eg peel, cores and pips. Bread. Tea leaves.

• Do not put meat, fish or cheese into your compost - they can attract rats and other pests.

⚠ Peat compost

Peat is formed naturally from rotted plants and is found in peat bogs. Once peat has been dug up for compost, it will take many years for it to form again. It is much better to make your own compost than use peat compost.

Sara and Marié's school in France have started using a new compost bin to dispose of their unwanted food.

➡ Action!

Sara   Marié

Make compost

• You'll need a compost bin with a lid. The bin has no bottom, and should be placed flat on soil to allow worms and other insects to get in.

• Add a mixture of uncooked food waste, leaves, grass clippings and weeds.

• Mix with cardboard egg boxes, brown paper. It will start to rot and get hot.

• Worms and beetles will start to break down the contents of your bin.

• When rich, dark brown compost develops at the bottom it can be used in the garden to make soil rich.

Safety

Wear gloves. Wash hands.

Fairtrade

Cheap food for us can mean that farmers in poor parts of the developing world are not getting a fair price for their food. Fairtrade products avoid this. They are sometimes more expensive. This is because the farmers have been given enough money to pay their workers a good wage to live on.

Different countries have their own Fairtrade labels, e.g:

UK

Guarantees a **better deal** for Third World Producers ®

FAIRTRADE

USA and Canada

FAIR TRADE CERTIFIED®

Look for this Mark on Fairtrade products.

Find out more about Fairtrade at: www.fairtrade.org.uk

The Fairtrade logo on food in our shops tells us that the farmers who produced the food are getting a fair deal when we buy it. Look for the Fairtrade logo when you go shopping.

Fairtrade produce

Fairtrade food you can buy includes fresh fruit, cocoa and chocolate, sugar, coffee, tea, rice herbs and spices, honey, nuts and snacks.

This farmer produces Fairtrade bananas. They are sold in supermarkets all over the world.

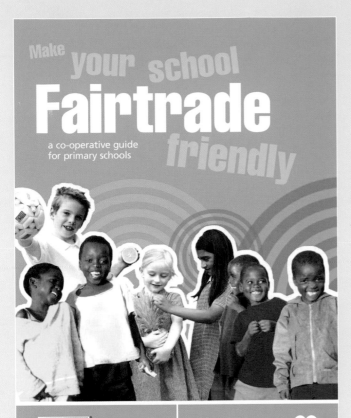

Make **your school**
Fairtrade
a co-operative guide
for primary schools
friendly

FAIRTRADE Guarantees a better deal for Third World Producers
Ask for Fairtrade products
www.fairtrade.org.uk

the co-operative college co op

Get your school to become a Fairtrade school by
only buying fairtrade products.

Rich/poor lunch

A rich/poor lunch will help you learn the
concept of "fair" and "unfair".
Everyone buys a numbered ticket for the
same price. Tickets are pulled out of a
hat. Some children get a slice of pizza
and and something sweet for desert,
while others just get a bowl of rice and
beans. Think about the fact that in some
parts of the world people have to
survive on a "poor lunch" every day of
their lives. Is this fair?

rich lunch

Challenge!

- Recognise the Fairtrade
  products logo.
- Change something you buy
  regularly to a Fairtrade product.
- Add more Fairtrade food to your
  shopping basket week by week and
  eat it in your packed lunch.
- Challenge your school to buy
  Fairtrade food for school lunches
  and the staff room.

poor lunch

Food festival

Holding a food festival is a way of sharing all you have learned about what is good for you and good for the planet with friends, family, other schools and the local community. Plan a festival that will inspire everyone to think about the food they eat and then make changes at home, at school or at the place where they work.

Action!

At your food festival:

- Sell cakes, bread and smoothies made by the cookery club.
- Give a cookery demonstration.
- Set up a stall with posters and information about Fairtrade and food miles.
- Sell produce from the school garden.
- Give guided tours of the vegetable garden.
- Invite everyone to share an eco-friendly school lunch.
- Have competitions, games and workshops.

Food festivals

These children in Morocco are taking part in a food festival. They are making food from all over the world for other people to eat and enjoy. This encourages others to see where food comes from and what good food should taste like.

Challenge!

- Hold a food festival.
- Invite people from the local community and family and friends.
- Plan a day of fun that everyone will remember.
- Follow it up and find out if anyone has made changes to the way they grow, buy, cook and eat their food.

Learn about food

Local farmers and organic and Fairtrade food suppliers often set up stalls at festivals and introduce themselves to the local community. This is a great way to learn more about good food.

A local farmers' market in the USA.

Cookery demonstration

Cookery clubs sometimes offer demonstrations for their favourite eco-friendly recipes. You could go along and get a chance to taste it and learn how to make it at home.

Fun at cookery club!

Index

The
Green
Team

Your Food

Sally Hewitt

W
FRANKLIN WATTS

First published in 2008 by
Franklin Watts
338 Euston Road
London NW1 3BH

Franklin Watts Australia
Level 17/207 Kent Street
Sydney NSW 2000

Editor: Jeremy Smith
Art director: Jonathan Hair
Design: Jason Anscomb

We would like to thank Bridget Ringdahl for use of
photographs and her text relating to Rocklands Primary,
South Africa.

Picture credits: Alamy: 8 all, 20b. Bridget Ringdahl: 14t, 20t,
22. Corbis: 3, 5, 14, 16t, 17 all. Fairtrade: 24 all, 25t.
istockphoto.com: 13b, 19b. Martin Luther King Junior School:
15. Mossbank School, Shetland: 12t. Plan International: 19t.
SIGN: 10-11 all. Shutterstock: 6-7 all, 9 all, 12bl & br, 12c, 21
all, 22, 23 all, 25cr & b. Stephanie Alexander Kitchen
Foundation: 18 all. Every attempt has been made to clear
copyright. Should there be any inadvertent omission please
apply to the publisher for rectification.

Dewey Classification: 941.085
ISBN: 978 0 7496 7934 7

Printed in China

Franklin Watts is a division of Hachette Children's
Books, an Hachette Livre UK company.